Let

Be

What

Is

Poetry on the Ways God
Breaks, Heals, and Shapes Us

Let Be What Is

Poetry on the Ways God Breaks, Heals,
and Shapes Us

by

Anna Michal

with illustrations by Jamie Crowley

Doug,

You saw me in my darkest hour
and told me to write a poem.
Consider this my thank-you note.

Love,
"George"

Contents

Instrument 8

Paralysis 10

Paradox 12

Guilt 14

Intuition 16

Motion 18

Heartbreak 20

Devastation 22

Sanctuary 24

Healing 26

Lullaby 28

Sight 30

Protection 32

Faithfulness 34

Crucifixion 36

Relief 38
Acceptance 40
Discovery 42
Ambition 44
Homecoming 46
Intercession 48
Photosynthesis 50
Justice 52
Receiving 54
Witness 56
Desire 58
Companionship 60
Aging 62
Vocation 64
Passage 66

Instrument

Whatever it is that's
Taking you,
Pushing you,
Chasing you,
Thrusting you,
Yes, forcing you
To cling to the heart of God,
Do not deny it.
Do not forget to be thankful for it.
Embrace it,
Accept it,
Forgive it for happening.
Though it may be
Choking you,
Killing you,
In the end, it will not succeed.
This is not to say it does not
Pain you,
Alter you,
Just that it cannot win.
It will, in fact, it must become a beauty.
Have you not heard our God redeems
Everything?

You may have
Heard this,
Read this,
But by the end of your life, your bones will
Know it.
And in the meantime, can you admit that
Though it
Burns you,
Hurts you,
Breaks you,
The reward of His closeness is greater still?
Perhaps you cannot say that yet.
My friend,
My loved one,
I promise,
I promise,
You will.

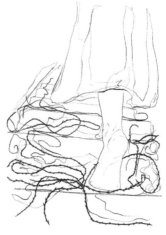

Paralysis

Sometimes, there is nothing left to do
But to let the pain course through you.
When you've read all the words you know are true,
When you know your friends really do love you,
And you cannot reverse pain with the truth.
It's okay that there is nothing left to do.
It's okay that up ahead bright days seem few.
It's okay that all your plans are fumbled and strewn.
Cry a thousand times if you must. It's not new.
God can take a crumpled, moody, dissonant you.

It's okay. You don't know what to do.

Paradox

Oh, my heart. What did you think?
"It Is Well" sings sweeter still in the pain from which
you shrink.

And that mountaintop for which you weep and pray?
Tears of the valley make it most precious when dark
gives way to day.

Do you feel you'll die in this despair?
Believe the saints who have gone before; you aren't
damaged beyond His repair.

And you are tired aren't you, so cast aside and worn?
Give Him some time to show you that hope can be
reborn.

Are you scared of God, my heart, because He lets you
bleed?
But you will find your God will break you to see that
you go free.

Guilt

Eve, Eve, Eve,
You get such a bad rap.
I'd have done no different
On a day like that.
Oh, Eve, Eve,
My mother, my blood,
The glory of women
Is not in what we've done.
Eve, oh Eve.
One fruit sold our souls,
Rape, anguish, murder-
We pay a heavy toll.
Eve, my sister,
Do you see your sisters cry?
Do not watch the violence-
Oh Eve, shield your eyes.
Eve, Eve, Eve,
Looking back from my mirror,
We all shoulder screams
We should never have to hear.
Eve, in my eyes,
Do not die in your despair,
Find in guilty living
The God who is there.
Eve, my beloved,
What have you done?
Do not hide your face,
For the Lover has come.

Eve, oh my soul,
Cry for Justice outpoured-
And when He arrives,
We weep no more.

Intuition

They say a woman should always listen
To her inward intuition,
But mine is little and very scared.
Spirit, have you any of yours to share?
If so, please teach mine what is true,
Assure my intuition that the surest thing is You.

Let Be What Is

Motion

It's the way of things-
The constant ebb and flow.
But I feel tired of saying goodbye,
And not ready for the next hello.
Sometimes, when the tide rolls out
With pieces of me in tow,
It almost feels unbearable -
The releasing, the letting go.
Moon and Stars of my inner night,
Who says it must be so,
Bathe me again in kindly light;
It's a tear-stained night here below.
Shine on, shine on,
You turn the waves, I know,
Lift my eyes to a better shore,
And see Your pilgrim home.

Let Be What Is

Heartbreak

You can hardly breathe from pain.
I know. I know. It pours when it rains.
Vivid remembrance strikes you like blows -
It hurts. I know. Oh, how well I know.
You say no reason to live is left,
But here is one: you still have breath.
The future is gone, and all your dreams too,
Well, yes, that may be true.
You have nothing, are nothing, you can't even stand.
Let Him do the standing if someone must stand.
Lie down, just lie down.
He will sit with you here on the ground.
Your heart is broken beyond all words.
Yes, language is inadequate, I'm sure.
Your insides are aflame, but you will learn -
It's okay. For a while they must burn.
You're broken, you have no more fight.
Yes. Yes, be still. You are right.
What will you do? What will you ever do?
There's nothing left. Let Jesus husband you.

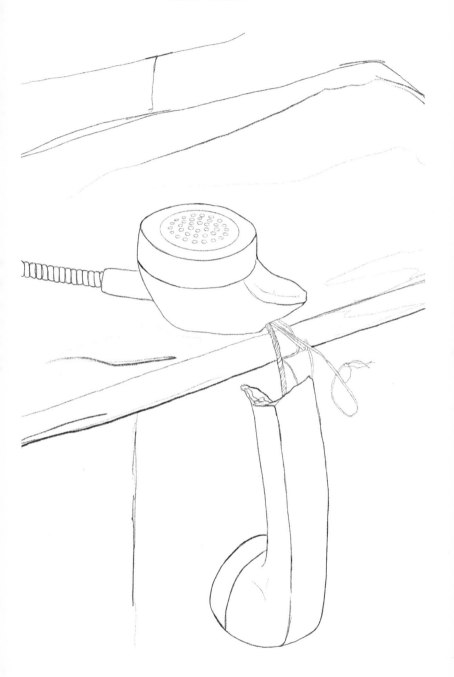

Devastation

I'm a writer with no words-
Jesus, pray for me.
My pleas, they seem unheard-
Jesus, pray for me.
My tears fail to express-
Jesus, pray for me.
My heart is shattered in my chest-
Jesus, pray for me.
Faltering, halting, my faith-
Jesus, pray for me.
Until I see your face-
Jesus, pray for me.

Sanctuary

I slipped my shoes off and curled
My frame onto my bed
Like an old dog, whose one year
Costs him seven in this world.
As maybe mine cost me.

Jesus touched me, and I turned
My soul onto her side
To reach out for Him, since none
Draw near and close like my Lord.
Lulled, held, I fell asleep.

Healing

The wind of winter has torn through my soul-
Oh, my Lord. It has been unforgiving and cold.
My heart has been broken, and viciously so,
My spirit is sagging from the ache in my bones.
But spring is arriving, or so someone said,
I sense dim hope through the fog in my head.
The fire is dying (though its coals still burn),
And I notice with interest the robin's return.
My eyes are swollen from tearful nights,
Yet the sun comforts me with pale morning light.
I've grown used to the darkness and my skin of hurt,
But a molting begins; You lift me up from the dirt.
I will never forget, and I can't be the same,
But hope takes shape; flowers whisper my name.
The iris, the crocus, they each know their place,
They respond to Your calling with magnificent grace.
Spring is not hindered; she keeps on with her coming.
And You keep on, with Your gentle loving.

Let Be What Is

Lullaby

Safety is not what I thought or wished it could be.
God's protection doesn't spare, but it guarantees-

I am safe.
No matter the sin that erupts from my heart,
Christ's blood covers all of me, not just a part.
I am safe.
When I'm blind with the pain of life's punishing bite,
It can steal everything, except me from His sight.
I am safe.
When I hate Him and wouldn't trust Him if I could,
He woos until my shaking fist admits that He is good.
I am safe.
When I'm done thrashing and fighting for my will,
Everlasting arms of love carry me still.
I am safe.
When my world collapses, when life has reached its end,
He weaves my ruins into artistry again.
I am safe.

The future may be more unsure, the past may pain me still,
But I can live this present breath in the safety of His will.

Sight

You can live with dysfunction,
But sooner or later it catches up.
The same could be said of healing.
This morning I scrunched my toes,
I felt my skin against the sheets,
I woke up feeling unexpectedly alive, myself.
The world was beautiful again.
You can cry Christ's name into the air,
You can look for Him everywhere,
And then, one day, unguarded,
Catch Him standing there.
He looks on and waits for you to see.
And when you do,
He is not the one who has changed.

Protection

Little spider veins of worry
Spread through my spirit's every curve,
Carrying fear all through me, and,
Like the birthmark crawling across my back,
Sometimes they surface for all to see.

What am I afraid of? Countless things,
Tangle upon tangle of wispy bloodlines.
But the main artery winds around and clings
To a warped, weary image of Christ. My Christ,
Lover of the weak, whom He covers with His wings.

I am most desperate for that shield.
I am shot through with need, ambivalence.
But, by what mercy can I question, doubt, heal,
And despite my suspicions, find protection?
This is proof to flickering faith; I am safe to yield.

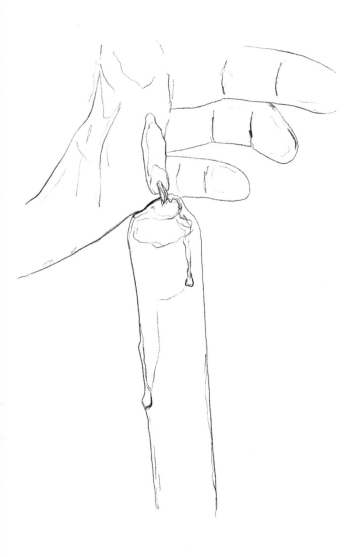

Faithfulness

Sit with me at the table, God.
My friends have gone, one-by-one,
To sleep, to play, to work.
By some mercy I am not tired,
I cannot laugh just now,
Nor do I have much ambition.
I have only the notion to sit by a fire
Everyone else has left.
And I'm feeling, if I may say it,
Rather lonely.
Sit with me and hold my hand.
Hold it with Your right hand,
The righteous one,
The one I've read will uphold me.

Crucifixion

I hope for forgiveness if I've hurt you with the
worst of me.
I have parts and places I'm still scared to let Jesus
touch.
I wish He'd brush by them unobservant and let
them be.
Healing is deep and difficult, harder than wound-
ing. Much.

I am sorry. Let me walk with Him a little more.
Give Him time.
These shards will be removed, but not by me. I've
tried.
The cross must do it, and my scars will make me
gentler and kind.
Then I'll gladly let you near. Touch my hands, my
feet, my side.

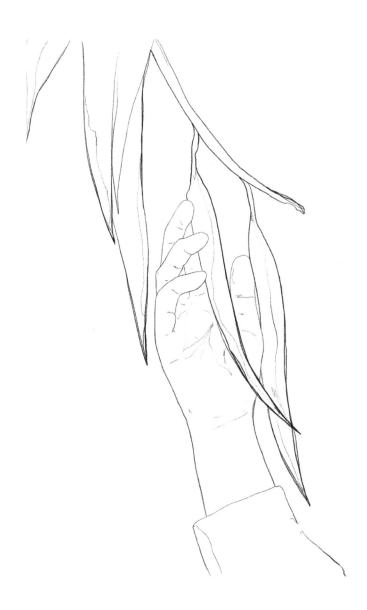

Relief

"He's never not shown up,"
I said to my friend
Who was scared.
And I was scared too,
So I decided to say something brave.
But that scared me all over again-
What if I was wrong?
I scanned my brain,
I searched my heart
In a panicky split second,
As if to say,
"Wait, was there a time?"
But instead of finding one,
I collided headlong with Him-
His Spirit, there, settled
Steadfast in my soul.
I breathed relief to be right.
Still there, still there,
My God. I wake,
From sleep or fear or both-
And I am still with You.

Acceptance

I no longer want to stifle my longings.
Let them rage.
Because of them I've found the God for
Whom desire is made.
I no longer wish to rewrite my story -
Even the scary parts.
I see now they're inked in love and
Lead me to His heart.
I no longer care about my path, or
Wish for one more grand.
When it's here, on this road, that
He offers me His hand.
I no longer wish I could be other, or
Struggle differently.
I know that in my body, with my crosses,
Jesus heals so beautifully.

Isn't this half the battle, accepting what's
real, what's true?
Having the grace and humility to say "yes"
and choose to be you?

Discovery

Wide-eyed girl, what do you find?
I find that before Him I was utterly blind.
Lost mind of a dreamer, what do you find?
I find His dreams are much greater than mine.
Fears and failures, what do you find?
I find that His gaze is tender and kind.
Ambivalent heart, what do you find?
I find that the cross is the one sure sign.
Wayward, reckless spirit, what do you find?
I find His fire; it hurts but refines.
Dear longing soul, what do you find?
I find love that fills the longer I dine.
Wounded, broken human, what do you find?
I find bruised, bloody messes He doesn't mind.
Woman so fragile, what do you find?
I find my dependence is by His design.
Anna, poor and needy, what do you find?
I find who I am: a branch in the Vine.

Ambition

You want to do great things,
Say great things,
Be great things.
But what if all God has is this?
You, sitting up against His side,
Him, convincing you?
Can it be enough to learn of Him
And not accomplish all that much?
Maybe being still makes room for motion.
After all,
Don't you think the loved are lovers?
Don't you think the safe are havens?
Don't you think the found are guides?

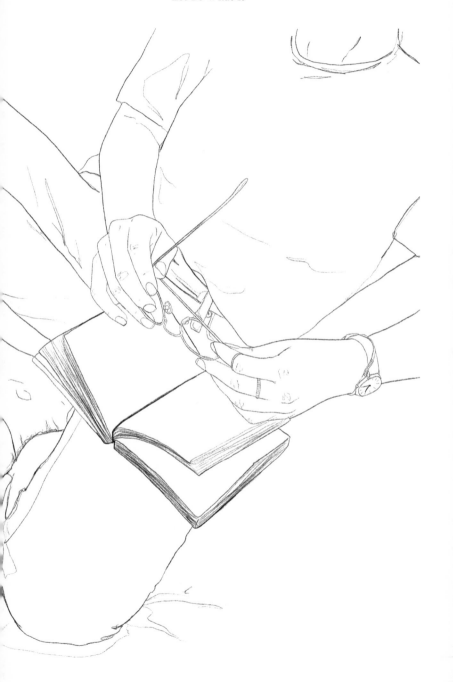

Homecoming

You, like coming home,
Where I can count on floorboards
Always creaking the same way
And sunspots warming my bones,
Are a relief. I enter.
Kindness draws me here.
It speaks of all we don't need to say-
I'm Yours. You're mine.
You'll stay.

Intercession

My friend is fighting things.
I hear pain in her voice,
I watch the way her eyes shift wearily,
And I know.
I try to speak tenderly,
To touch as needed,
But *I love yous* from me
Can only go so far.
She has entered regions I have known,
Wilderness I'll know again,
But cannot now enter with her.
Only God resides there.
My heart is pained.
She must wrestle with One
Who will have His will
At any cost.
A good, good will, but one requiring
Gethsemane.
I have settled myself at the gate,
To wait. Wait.
3 days? Months? Years?
I do not know.

I pray she will cry out,
That she will allow herself humanity.
I pray she will weep, and then,
I pray that she will come to drink
Whatever cup He offers.
I pray to watch.
I pray to stay
Awake.

Photosynthesis

The way light shifts mystifies me.
As do God's affections.

Now
White, soft, pure, gentle,
Healing, cleansing,
Comfortable, and kind-

And now
Bright, harsh, blinding,
Piercing, overwhelming,
Exposing all.

Regardless, the fern unfurls, and thrives.
And I, by the Lover's touch, arise.

Justice

A friend of mine is crying on my doorstep,
Another, fuming on my phone.
First, I think we should remind ourselves-
Thoughts are worse when you're alone.
And then we should remember:
The world is crumbling,
But no more so now than ever.
This is not a call to do nothing,
This is not a call to do something,
This is just an appeal
To keep in mind that if the sky falls,
It is because it has always been falling,
And that whatever good thing
Action or inaction may accomplish,
We cannot keep it in place.
Nor can we prevent
The real work from being done.
Jesus still spins His prayer shawls,
Still holds up His holy, holed hands,
Still gathers prayers in His arms
Before the eyes of God,
Mediating all, ministering to all,
Swaddling oppressed hearts,
Seeing the hearts of oppressors,
Offering them corners of His covering,
Fitting them for justice.

I tell myself and my friends,
"Don't be extreme and lose it."
"Don't be asleep and miss it."
Just open your eyes, your soul.
Let the neighbor nearest you
See your naked spirit
Where the Spirit of the sewing
Christ resides.
This will be enough.
Already, it's enough.

Receiving

"Easy, bud." I murmur.
I'm not sure
Who is fidgeting more,
My nephew, or the frog
Clutched in his clammy hand.
"Be gentle," I say.
He is wracked with emotion,
Squeezing the frog one moment,
Throwing it the next.
I cup my hands around his;
He needs a little help.
His body trembles.
"It won't hurt you."
He watches with amazement,
With a mixture of
Delight and uncertainty.
He must learn,
Among many things,
That gifts are best received
Reverently, with care,
Not with greedy squeezing
Or fearful pitching,
Which heighten desire
Never to satisfy it.
I understand him.
"Hold still, it's okay, hon."
He must learn to hold his gifts.
He's not the only one.

Witness

Some would call Scripture
A love story, a history book, a plan,
An explanation;
All are fair descriptions.
But I find it best described
As a witness,
A record of reality,
A headline reading:
"THINGS AS THEY ARE"-
Too awful, too bloody to deny,
Too good, too holy to fathom.
And blessed is he who swallows it,
Who wakes to drink of it,
Who gives his whole self to its nourishment.
For therein is what is,
Therein glimpse I Am,
Therein see something,
The one thing,
In all this mess that is true.
Therein may a soul cry out,
And if he be not answered,
Find at least his scales removed.

Desire

Christ, dig me an ear. Peel open my eyes.
Whatever You do, don't let my faith die.
Sift my soul; make me as wheat.
Purge my heart near the raging heat.
Christ, hold up my head; hold me in place,
So when suffering comes I won't turn away.
But above all else, Lord, let the cup pass.
Remember, my God, that I am like grass.
Lord, what I've prayed for I fear to live-
I have limped before from gifts that You give.
But still I pray it, and I wait for Your grace;
I will look on horrors if that's what it takes.
If life's going to change and tear me apart,
May it alter my vision to see Your heart.
Who wants their turn on the humble cross?
Have mercy, my Christ, as I pay the cost.
I tremble, I tremble, but have come to know -
Wherever You've gone is where I will go.
This gospel has touched me. I've tasted too much.
I've seen you are Lord; I love You as such.
Darkness exists to make much of the light-
Christ, I must have You. Plunge me in night.

Companionship

If my arms feel tender to your frame,
If my words seem aptly fit,
If my eyes pour forth a loving flame,
And the occasion, I rise to it,

Do not think me great.

If I touch your fear until it's tame,
If I know when you weep to just sit,
If I shoulder weight when you are lame
And caress where you've been hit,

Do not think me knowing.

Think me broken, think me same,
Think me familiar with your pit,
Think me needy in life's cruel game,
Think me friends with tears and grit.

But do not think me complete.

Do not think me strong, think this:
Think God fills me with love at your name,
Think He tailors His yoke to fit,
Think He is healing whatever is maimed -

If you need living proof, I'll be it.

Aging

Let it not be a shock, a crisis, when
The day comes that I can no longer
Gather ingredients to bake bread,
Pick up a pen to express myself,
Or really, create anything anymore.
Let me not fret or complain
When no amount of lotion
Nor oceans of water can smooth
And rejuvenate my tired face and skin,
And in the night I rise, sleepless and old.
Let me not panic or bend too far awry
When friends who have stood by
All my life must go their own way
With God and say goodbye, while I linger -
Here to receive whatever graces are left.
Let me leave with Him all these.
Passing are my ideas, body, loved ones, and
All else I long to bring me personhood.
I forget that they are near to me
But are not me - until the mercy of loss.
Let me embrace whatever
Brings me face to face with the
Definer, Namer, and Shaper of my essence,
Whose love leads to self-discovery:
I begin and end inside His arms alone.

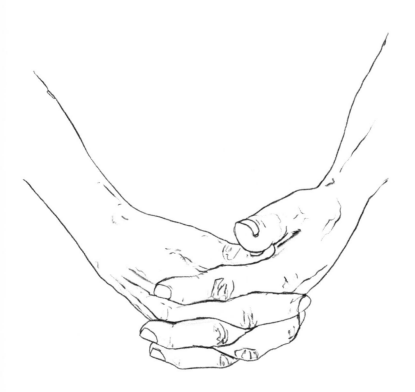

Vocation

God,
Riveting, all-consuming,
Does not let me pass Him by.
I must write and describe,
From the cleft I've been assigned,
His glory passing by.
Will I do Him adequate justice with words-
The justice He is due?
No,
But to stop to wonder or grieve
Would cause the rocks to cry too.
This is my madness, my poison,
Which I'll drink until I die,
My great failure and my passion,
God help me,
The point of my life-
To try.

Let Be What Is

Passage

What am I?
Just a creature bound
By time and space,
Continuing in grace, but ever so
Slowly.
It is something holy though,
I think,
For a heart to sink
In wishing it were more.

A soul must kiss
The dusty road a hundred times
Or more,
To find blessing in
The humble way of the One
It's walking toward.

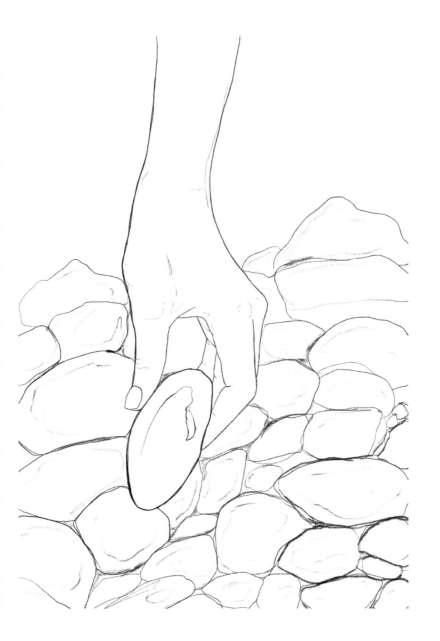

Anna Michal works as a professional copywriter and is co-author of *Fearless: Facing the Future Confidently with Relational Estate Planning®*, but creative writing is her first love. Outside of writing poetry and spiritual essays, Anna spends her time reading, hiking, and experimenting with fresh ingredients in her kitchen.

Jamie Crowley is a self-taught artist who was born and raised in the Shenandoah Valley. Over the years, she has worked with several different mediums but has found that digital art is her favorite. When she isn't creating, you can find Jamie drinking chai, thrifting, or taking long drives while blaring Jon Bellion.

Let Be What Is: Poetry on the Ways God Breaks, Heals, and Shapes Us

Cover design: Madeleine Long //https://www.maddielong.com
Interior design: Madeleine Long//https://www.maddielong.com

First printing 2021
Printed in the United States of America
Trade Paperback ISBN: 978-1-7367552-0-4